Read for a Better World™

TOYS AND GAMES
A Look at
THEN and NOW

D1736684

PERCY LEED

GRL Consultant, Diane Craig, Certified Literacy Specialist

Lerner Publications ◆ Minneapolis

Educator Toolbox

Reading books is a great way for kids to express what they're interested in. Before reading this title, ask the reader these questions:

What do you think this book is about? Look at the cover for clues.

What do you already know about toys and games in the past?

What do you want to learn about toys and games in the past?

Let's Read Together

Encourage the reader to use the pictures to understand the text.

Point out when the reader successfully sounds out a word.

Praise the reader for recognizing sight words such as *at* and *in*.

TABLE OF CONTENTS

Toys and Games Then and Now 4

Toys and Games Then and Now

Kids love to play.
New toys and games
come out all the time.

Do you have any toys made at home?

6

THEN

Dolls were made at home.

NOW

Dolls are sold in stores.

Kids played with wooden blocks.

NOW

Kids play with plastic blocks.

THEN

Kids rode rocking horses.

NOW

Kids ride bikes.

THEN

Kids played with marbles at school.

NOW

Kids play on playgrounds at school.

THEN

Toy trains were moved by hand.

What other toys move by themselves?

NOW

Toy trains move by themselves.

15

THEN

Kids played jacks.

NOW

Kids play video games.

What stuffed animals do you have?

THEN

Kids hugged teddy bears.

NOW

Kids hug all kinds of stuffed animals.

There are many new toys
and games today.

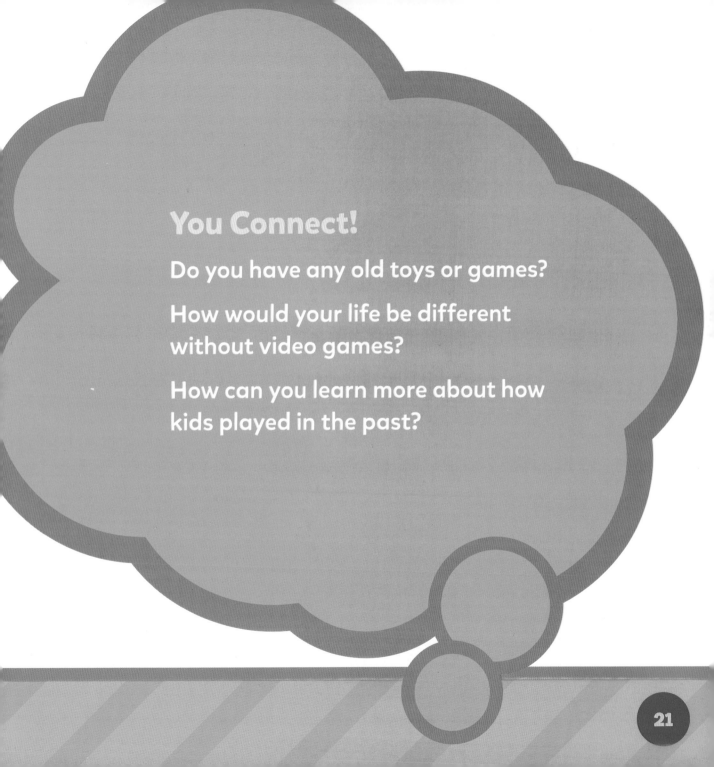

You Connect!

Do you have any old toys or games?

How would your life be different without video games?

How can you learn more about how kids played in the past?

Social and Emotional Snapshot

Student voice is crucial to building reader confidence. Ask the reader:

What is your favorite part of this book?

What is something you learned from this book?

Did this book remind you of any toys you've played with?

Opportunities for social and emotional learning are everywhere. How can you connect the topic of this book to the SEL competencies below?

Relationship Skills
Self-Awareness
Social Awareness

Photo Glossary

jacks

marbles

playground

rocking horse

Learn More

Berne, Emma Carlson. *Toys and Games*. Minneapolis: Bearport Publishing, 2023.

Dinmont, Kerry. *Toys and Games Past and Present*. Minneapolis: Lerner Publications, 2019.

Smibert, Angie. *Video Games from Then to Now*. Mankato, MN: Amicus, 2020.

Index

Photo Acknowledgments

The images in this book are used with the permission of: © RichVintage/iStockphoto, pp. 4–5; © Everett Collection/Shutterstock Images, pp. 6, 18; © RgStudio/iStockphoto, p. 7; © Library of Congress, pp. 8, 12, 14, 16, 23 (jacks, marbles); © Fly View Productions/iStockphoto, p. 9; © Wikimedia Commons, pp. 10, 23 (rocking horse); © FatCamera/iStockphoto, p. 11; © fstop123/iStockphoto, pp. 13, 23 (playground); © modchan/Shutterstock Images, p. 15; © PeopleImages/iStockphoto, p. 17; © ozgurcankaya/iStockphoto, p. 19; © Wavebreakmedia/iStockphoto, p. 20.

Cover Photographs: © George Marks/iStockphoto (inset); © Riska/iStockphoto (video games)

Design Elements: Mighty Media, Inc.

Lerner Publications Company
An imprint of Lerner Publishing Group, Inc.
241 First Avenue North
Minneapolis, MN 55401 USA

For reading levels and more information, look up this title at www.lernerbooks.com.

Main body text set in Mikado a Medium.
Typeface provided by Hannes von Doehren.

Library of Congress Cataloging-in-Publication Data

Names: Leed, Percy, 1968-author.
Title: Toys and games : a look at then and now / Percy Leed.
Description: Minneapolis : Lerner Publications, [2024] | Series: Read about the past (Read for a better world) | Includes bibliographical references and index. | Audience: Ages 5–8 | Audience: Grades K–1 | Summary: "What did children do for fun and entertainment long ago? Readers can find out in this book filled with exciting photographs to show what toys and games were like in the past"—Provided by publisher.
Identifiers: LCCN 2022037111 (print) | LCCN 2022037112 (ebook) | ISBN 9781728491493 (library binding) | ISBN 9798765603550 (paperback) | ISBN 9781728499543 (ebook)
Subjects: LCSH: Toys—History—Juvenile literature. | Toys—Pictorial works—Juvenile literature. | Games—History—Juvenile literature. | Games—Pictorial works—Juvenile literature.
Classification: LCC GV1218.5 .L425 2023 (print) | LCC GV1218.5 (ebook) | DDC 790.1/33—dc23/eng/20220825

LC record available at https://lccn.loc.gov/2022037111
LC ebook record available at https://lccn.loc.gov/2022037112

Manufactured in the United States of America
2-1012475-51098-4/2/2025